Uses for

Reynolds Wrap®
Aluminum
Foil

Over 100
Helpful
Household
Hints

Publications International, Ltd.

Publications
International, Ltd.

Contents

On a Roll with
Reynolds Wrap® Foil

When Reynolds Wrap® Aluminum Foil was introduced in 1947, it was advertised as "the pure aluminum foil for 1,001 kitchen miracles." Homemakers instantly fell in love with the versatile material and found new kitchen uses for it every day—and what made aluminum foil so useful back then is still true today. It's moisture-proof, odor-proof, and grease-proof and can be molded to any shape you like. It withstands high heat and extreme cold, making it perfect for everything from grilling to freezer storage.

Today, Reynolds Wrap Foil is still one of the best materials for cooking and food storage in the kitchen, but you'll find uses for it throughout the house. We've gathered some favorite ways to use it indoors and outdoors!

In this book you'll find more than 100 ways to put foil to work for you. Whether you're painting in the workshop or transplanting seedlings in the garden, foil is an essential tool that can make almost any household task less taxing. You'll also find tips for using foil to decorate for a special occasion, to make travel easier, and even some ways that using foil can save you money. We've also selected some of the best ways foil can save you time and trouble in the kitchen or when barbecuing at the grill. We even found room for some of our favorite recipes for cooking with foil.

Once you've seen these incredible tips for using foil around the house, we're sure you'll agree that foil is one of the most adaptable tools in the entire house.

Reynolds Wrap Foil is available in a variety of widths and thicknesses to accommodate just about any task. For wrapping and covering, use standard Reynolds Wrap Foil. For those tough jobs like lining pans, freezing, or grilling, use Reynolds Wrap Heavy Duty Foil. When you have sticky messes, use Reynolds Wrap® Non-Stick Foil—it has a special coating on one side so even the stickiest foods like barbecue chicken lift right off. And the newest member of the family, Reynolds Wrap® Foil from 100% Recycled Aluminum, is perfect for people looking for simple ways to show they care about the environment.

Chapter 1

Cooking & Food

Reynolds Wrap® Foil is an indispensable tool in the kitchen. For years professional chefs and home cooks alike have relied on Reynolds Wrap Foil to help with everything from keeping their stoves and ovens clean to protecting frozen foods from freezer burn. But there is no reason to stop there; a little foil can save you a lot of time and trouble in the kitchen. Whether prepping ingredients for a dish you'll prepare later, reheating appetizers as the party gets started, or helping clean up afterwards, foil is one kitchen secret everyone can share.

PREPARE TO PARTY

Throwing a party? Follow these simple tips to spend more time with your guests, not in the kitchen with the food.

Food Prep

Chop, shred, or grate similar ingredients for multiple recipes at the same time, then wrap with foil and refrigerate. Foil keeps food odors from transferring to other foods.

Advanced Appetizers

Make up appetizers in advance, wrap them tightly in heavy duty foil, and freeze. When company arrives, just pop frozen appetizers into the oven. Baking for most appetizers takes about 20 minutes from the freezer.

Share Oven Space

Reheat several types of frozen appetizers together in one pan, each on a separate sheet of foil with the edges turned up. The foil keeps the pans clean and prevents juices and flavors from mingling.

Fresh Baked (and Frozen) Bread

Avoid the last-minute rush—bake breads or rolls ahead of time. Wrap tightly in foil and freeze. Freeze up to 2 months in advance.

TURKEY TIPS

Roasting a whole turkey is challenging even without all the details and other dishes for a festive meal. Use a little foil to simplify roasting a turkey for the holidays or any other time of year.

Rapid Roasting

 To speed up turkey roasting time, completely wrap the turkey in heavy duty foil and cook in a 450°F oven. Turn back the foil during the last 30 minutes to brown. *(See Foil Wrapped Roasted Turkey, page 9.)*

Turkey Tent

 For a picture-perfect roasted turkey, crease a foil sheet and place it loosely over the turkey like a tent. Remove after 1 hour. Non-stick foil won't stick to or tear the turkey skin, making a great presentation.

IN THE OVEN

Baked-on messes are no fun to clean up. Save yourself the trouble by not making them at all.

Keep Your Coat On

 Crumb coatings stick to the food, not the pan, if it's lined with non-stick foil. Foods like fish or chicken fingers are easily turned over without falling apart or losing their crust.

FOIL WRAPPED ROASTED TURKEY

REYNOLDS WRAP® Heavy Duty Foil

8 to 24 pound turkey, thawed

Vegetable oil

Preheat oven to 450°F. Remove neck and giblets from turkey; rinse turkey and pat dry. If desired, loosely stuff turkey. Brush skin with vegetable oil.

Tear off a sheet of 18-inch Reynolds Wrap® Heavy Duty Foil 2½ times as long as the turkey. Place turkey lengthwise in center of foil. Close foil loosely, overlapping the ends. Turn up short sides of foil to hold in juices. Do not seal airtight. Place in roasting pan at least 2 inches deep. Insert meat thermometer through foil into thickest part of inner thigh, not touching bone.

Roast turkey until meat thermometer reads 180°F following approximate roasting times in chart below. For stuffed turkey, add 30 minutes to roasting time. To brown turkey, open and turn back foil 30 minutes before end of roasting. For easy slicing, cover turkey with foil and let stand 15 minutes.

Makes 10 to 30 servings (depending on size of turkey)

TURKEY SIZE	COOKING TIME
8 to 12 pounds	1½ to 2¼ hours
12 to 16 pounds	2¼ to 2¾ hours
16 to 20 pounds	2¾ to 3¼ hours
20 to 24 pounds	3¼ to 3¾ hours

REYNOLDS KITCHEN TIP: Estimate 1 pound per person for generous servings with leftovers.

Finer Fish

Wrap a whole fish in foil just before baking, adding fresh herbs and other seasonings to taste. Place a cookie sheet beneath the foil-wrapped fish for support. The fish will stay moist and tender, and cleanup is a snap.

Better Broiling

To avoid the hassles of scrubbing, line both parts of broiler pans with non-stick foil. Cut slits at the rack openings to allow drippings to drain away while broiling.

Easy as (Pizza) Pie

Wrap leftover pizza in non-stick foil. When you're ready to reheat, simply open the foil and heat in the oven on the same foil sheet. The crust gets crisp and melted cheese won't stick!

Keep Your Oven Clean

Place foil a few inches larger than your baking pan on a lower oven rack. Turn up all the edges to catch any spills. Be sure heat can circulate around the foil. (To prevent damage to the oven, do not use foil to line the bottom of oven.)

BAKING BETTER GOODIES

Making oven-baked treats is so much faster and easier with the help of a few sheets of foil.

Faster Cookies

To speed up cookie baking, prepare dough as directed by your favorite recipe. Portion it out onto sheets of non-stick foil the same size as your cookie sheets. Slide a foil sheet onto a cookie sheet and bake as directed. As the cookies are baked, just slide off the entire foil sheet and its baked cookies, and slide the next sheet of cookie dough on. There's no waiting between batches, and hardly any cleanup.

Perfect Pie Crust

To prevent pie crusts from overbrowning, make a foil pie ring shield. Fold a 12-inch foil square into quarters. Cut out the center and round off the edges, leaving a 2-inch-wide ring. Unfold the ring and place it over the pie. Remove the foil ring for the final 20 minutes of baking time.

Prettier Pie

Jazz up store-bought pumpkin pie with pastry cut-outs. Use cookie cutters to cut leaf shapes from refrigerated pie crusts. Lightly draw leaf veins with a knife. Place the leaf shapes on a foil-lined cookie sheet, adding small balls of foil under shapes to make leaves curl. Bake per the crust directions; cool. Place on pie.

Cut Brownies and Bars Easily

Line a pan with non-stick foil. Add batter or dough to the foil-lined pan and bake as directed. When the brownies or bar cookies are cool, lift them by the foil from the pan and place onto a cutting board. Fold down the edges of the foil, and cut into individual brownies or bars. *(See Chocolate Chip Toffee Bars, page 13.)*

Better (and Easier) Than Store Bought

Choose one great cookie recipe that you can easily mass-produce. Bake a few batches and cool completely. Divide the baked cookies in quantities of one dozen and wrap in foil. Freeze them for holiday parties, or invite friends for a cookie swap.

Easy and Elegant

When you want fancy cookies in a hurry, place store-bought cookies on a cookie sheet lined with foil and drizzle with icing to create a pretty zigzag effect on the cookies. All the mess is on the foil, so there's no cleanup.

CHOCOLATE CHIP TOFFEE BARS

REYNOLDS WRAP® Non-Stick Foil

1 package (18 ounces) refrigerated chocolate chip cookie dough

1 can (14 ounces) sweetened condensed milk

1 cup almond toffee bits

1 cup sweetened flaked coconut, divided

½ cup sliced almonds, divided

1 cup semi-sweet chocolate chips

Preheat oven to 350°F. Line 13×9×2-inch baking pan with Reynolds Wrap Non-Stick Foil with non-stick (dull) side toward food, extending foil over sides of pan.

Press cookie dough evenly into bottom of foil-lined pan. Bake 15 to 17 minutes or until lightly browned. Remove from oven.

Combine sweetened condensed milk, toffee bits, ½ cup coconut and ¼ cup almonds. Spread evenly over hot baked cookie dough. Sprinkle chocolate chips, remaining coconut and almonds over mixture. Return to oven.

Continue baking 20 to 25 minutes until bubbly and coconut is light golden brown. Cool in pan on a wire rack. Use foil to lift bars from pan onto a cutting board. Cut into bars.

Makes 36 bars

Bagel Baker's Dozen

 Keep bagels fresh and tasty by wrapping them with foil. Wrap sliced bagels individually in foil. Write the name of the flavor on the foil with a permanent marker and freeze. Unwrap, defrost, and eat!

Chocolate Shells

 Chocolate shells make a very elegant dessert. Mold non-stick foil (dull side out) to the back of cleaned seashells. Spread melted chocolate over foil-covered shells and chill. Carefully peel foil from chocolate. *(See Chocolate Dessert Shells, page 15.)*

CLEVER KITCHEN TIPS

Foil is great for so many other kitchen uses.

Just a Splash

 To make a sprinkler top for vinegar or oil bottles, just mold a piece of foil over the bottle opening. Secure the top with a rubber band, then punch small holes in the foil.

Lost Twist Ties

To replace a missing twist tie, just tear off a strip of foil and wind it into a rope. Wrap the foil rope around bag or package and twist to hold in place.

CHOCOLATE DESSERT SHELLS

REYNOLDS WRAP® Non-Stick Foil

¾ cup semi-sweet chocolate chips

2 teaspoons shortening

Orange or raspberry sherbet

Vanilla ice cream

Cut four 6-inch squares of Reynolds Wrap Non-Stick Foil. Press foil over back of four 4- to 5-inch baking shells or seashells with non-stick (dull) side facing out. Turn under excess foil. Place shells on non-stick, foil-lined cookie sheet with non-stick (dull) side facing up.

Microwave chocolate chips and shortening in microwave-safe bowl on HIGH, 1 to 2 minutes, until chocolate is soft. Stir until smooth. Coat shells with chocolate; refrigerate at least 1 hour.

Remove baking shells carefully, leaving foil backing on chocolate shells. Peel foil from chocolate shells by placing chocolate side down on serving plate and gently peeling off foil.

Fill each shell with small scoops of sherbet and/or ice cream. Serve immediately.

Makes 4 servings

Chapter 2

Kitchen

No kitchen is complete without a full roll of Reynolds Wrap® Foil. You'll find it is an indispensable tool for helping you keep things clean. Scrub dirty pots and pans until they sparkle, or even protect your cookbooks from splatters and spots. You'll also find unexpected, but hassle-free, ways to use foil to save time and effort in the kitchen. Learn how to quickly make some of these temporary tools and gadgets and you'll be sure to always have a solution to any kitchen dilemma.

KITCHEN TIPS AND GADGETS

Can't find your favorite kitchen gadget? Make your own with these clever tips.

Customized Funnels

Foil can be shaped into funnels of any size or shape for use in pouring into small-mouthed bottles.

Jar Tops

Temporary tops for bottles or jars can be made quickly and simply from squares or circles of foil. Crimp tightly around top.

Extra-Large Mixing Bowl

When tossing a large salad or mixing turkey stuffing, line a large sink or pan with foil to serve as an extra-large bowl.

Easy Vegetable Steamer

Make your own vegetable steamer with a saucepan filled with 2 to 4 inches of water. Poke holes in a sheet of foil large enough to fit the saucepan. Mold to the top of the pan, crimping the edges. Depress the center slightly to form a well. Heat the water to boiling. Place the vegetables on the foil sheet and cover with the saucepan lid. Cook until the vegetables are crisp-tender.

KEEP IT CLEAN

Let foil help keep your kitchen clean and pristine. Wrap any items you're concerned about in foil and they're instantly safe from spills and dust.

Keep Your Counter Clean

Make a sandwich or wrap directly on a sheet of foil; then, wrap it up in the same sheet. You'll save time cleaning kitchen counters on a busy morning. *(See Veggie Pita Wraps, page 19.)*

Wall Shield

Protect your walls from stove-top splatter. Foil makes a convenient temporary shield for the backsplash behind your stove or range. Just wipe it clean, or even better, take it down when you finish cooking and toss it straight into your recycling bin.

Clean Drawers and Shelves

Keep pantries and cabinets spic and span with a simple, easy-to-install foil lining on shelves and in drawers. Since foil is impervious to liquids, a simple wipe with a damp cloth or sponge is all it takes to clean even sticky, drippy messes like spilled corn syrup or cooking oil. Change foil regularly to keep your drawers and shelves dust- and mess-free.

VEGGIE PITA WRAPS

4   sheets REYNOLDS WRAP® Foil

4   4-inch tortillas

½   cup garden vegetable cream cheese spread

    Curly leaf lettuce

1   medium cucumber, sliced lengthwise

4   slices mozzarella cheese

¼   cup sliced almonds (optional)

Place Reynolds Wrap Foil sheets on countertop as surface to make wrap sandwiches.

Place a tortilla on each foil sheet.

Spread 2 tablespoons cheese spread onto each tortilla. Top each with lettuce, cucumber slices, tomato and cheese. Sprinkle with almonds, if desired. Roll up tortilla, enclosing filling.

Wrap filled tortilla, seams-side down, in foil. Repeat to make four sandwiches. Refrigerate 30 minutes or until serving time

Makes 4 servings

Hot Pads

A heavy piece of cardboard (or even a magazine) covered with foil makes a practical and attractive mat for hot dishes. Use as is, or have the kids decorate the foil with permanent markers or stickers and labels for an extra home-style touch.

Cookbook Cover

You value all the investments you've made in your cookbooks, so protect them when you place them in harms way. A neat cover of foil keeps your cookbooks safe from stains while using them.

Scouring Pots and Pans

Stubborn messes are easily scoured out of pots and pans when you crumple foil into a fist-sized ball. Scrub with plenty of soap and hot water as you normally do, and watch even baked on residues come clean. For best results, use this technique for steel, aluminum and even glass pots, pans, and baking dishes, but not on cookware with non-stick coatings or those made from relatively soft materials like copper.

Lid Liners

Save a step and line the inside of the lid of a pot or pan with foil, especially when you're preparing foods that tend to splatter. No more scrubbing the inside of the lids when you're done; just recycle the foil.

SWEET TREATS

Let foil help ease the hassle of making homemade sweets and desserts.

Pie Crust Roller

If pie crust dough becomes unmanageably soft while rolling it out, wrap the partially rolled dough in foil and place in the freezer for a few minutes to chill. Unwrap, then roll to desired thickness.

Cake Decorating Tube

Perk up your cakes with this fancy (but fun) decorating technique. Fold a square of foil diagonally in half to form a large triangle. Starting along one short side, roll into a tight cone. Fill cone with frosting and seal large end. Snip tip of cone to create opening of desired size. Gently squeeze cone to force frosting out opening; use to decorate cake as desired.

Unique Tart Shells

Unusual and attractive pastry shells for sweet and even savory tarts can be easily made with foil. Cut circles, squares, or triangle foil shapes. Then cut matching shapes in pastry. Place the pastry shapes on the corresponding foil shape. With your thumb and finger, turn up the edges of both foil and pastry, pinching as the shape requires. Lift onto cookie sheets and bake as the recipe directs.

Chapter 3

Grilling

Grill masters know Reynolds Wrap® Foil is an indispensable tool that makes grilling great food easy. Keep a roll of Reynolds Wrap® Heavy Duty Foil with your other barbecue supplies and you'll be ready to grill up the good stuff any day of the week. Add a roll of Reynolds Wrap® Non-Stick Foil and even the stickiest foods like saucy barbecue chicken, delicate foods like fresh fish, and hard-to-grill items like asparagus will turn out better than ever.

LINE GRILL GRATES

Lining grill grates helps keep the grill clean. Use a grilling fork (or other large serving fork) to punch holes for drainage in a sheet of foil before placing the foil on the preheated grill. Food ready to serve? Leave the foil in place until it's cool enough to handle, then just discard. There's almost nothing left to clean up! Or you can line the grates of public grills in parks or picnic areas to ensure a clean surface anytime and anywhere you're ready to cook out.

Save Small Foods

 Keep small foods like shrimp and scallops from falling through the grill grate by lining it with foil.

Keep Foods from Sticking

Lining a grill grate with non-stick foil can help keep grilled food looking and tasting great. Delicate foods like fish fillets can be turned and flipped without falling apart. Foods like barbecued chicken or glazed pork chops that are basted with sticky sauces lift right off the grate.

Don't Burn the Burgers

Grill hamburgers on foil-lined grates to keep your burgers from sticking to the grate. It also helps prevent flare-ups from charring your patties.

A Better Way to Skin a Fish

Grill fish skinside down on a grill grate prepared with foil. Grill as directed by your favorite recipe. The skin will stick to the foil for the easiest way ever to skin a fish.

MAKE DIY FOIL GRILL PANS

Do-It-Yourself (DIY) Foil Grill Pans offer a simple way to save loads of time cleaning your grill. Place a pan the size and shape of the Foil Grill Pan you wish to make upside down on a counter. Mold two sheets of heavy duty foil to the outside of the pan. Remove the pan. Now just crimp the edges of the foil sheets together for added strength. Place on a tray to support it (especially once you fill it with food) and to transport it to and from the grill.

Grilling Vegetables

Make DIY Foil Grill Pans for vegetables. They'll be easy to turn and won't fall through the grill grate. *(See Grilled Marinated Vegetables, page 25.)*

GRILLED MARINATED VEGETABLES

REYNOLDS WRAP® Non-Stick Foil

1 small green bell pepper, cut into thin strips

1 small red or yellow bell pepper, cut into thin strips

1 small red onion, thinly sliced

1 package (8 ounces) fresh baby portobello mushrooms, halved

2 tablespoons chopped fresh basil or 1 tablespoon chopped fresh rosemary

3 tablespoons balsamic vinegar

2 tablespoons olive oil

2 cloves garlic, minced

Salt and black pepper to taste

Preheat grill to medium-high.

Combine vegetables, basil, vinegar, oil, garlic, salt and black pepper in a large bowl. Cover with Reynolds Wrap Non-Stick Foil and marinate at room temperature 15 to 20 minutes. Place vegetables in an even layer in a Reynolds Do-It-Yourself (DIY) Foil Grill Pan (see page 24). Slide onto grill grate.

Grill 8 to 10 minutes in covered grill, turning frequently, until vegetables are crisp-tender. Slide foil pan from grill onto a cookie sheet to transport from the grill.

Makes 4 servings

Another Idea for Keeping it Clean

 Grilling even some of your meal in foil pans helps to keep the grill clean. This is especially true for marinated foods which can leave a sticky mess on your grill grates. Grill pans can also keep foods with different cooking times separate when you're grilling them all at once, or when there may be cross contamination issues with adding foods to the grill at different times (such as when adding fish or chicken to a grill where you are already cooking corn-on-the-cob).

Indirect Benefits

Shape a DIY Foil Grill Pan over a 13×9×2-inch baking dish to use for indirect grilling larger cuts of meat on a charcoal grill. Place the Foil Grill Pan in the center of the lower grate of the grill. Arrange lit charcoal on either side of the Foil Grill Pan. Now just place the food to be grilled on the grate directly over the Foil Grill Pan and you're ready to slow-roast it to savory perfection.

When Less is More

Cookouts are more fun when there is less to clean up afterwards, so why dirty another dish just for barbecue sauce? Shape foil over small bowls using the same technique described above for DIY Foil Grill Pans to make disposable containers for barbecue sauce.

PACKET COOKING

Reynolds Quick & Easy Packet Cooking is an easy way to lock in the nutrients and flavor when grilling. Simply place ingredients in the center of a long sheet of foil. Bring up foil sides. Double fold top and ends to seal packet, leaving room for heat circulation inside.

Special Orders are No Problem

 Let everyone assemble their own packet so they can make it just the way they like it. Write names on packets with permanent markers (this maybe easier to do if you write on the foil before folding it into a packet).

Get All Steamed Up

For perfect crisp-tender veggies add 1 or 2 ice cubes to a packet containing just vegetables. The melting ice will provide just the right amount of moisture and steam to cook the vegetables perfectly.

Sides on the Side

If you're already planning to grill your main course, why not make a little extra room on the grill and cook your whole meal at once? Place a packet of buttered, seasoned potatoes or vegetables next to your steaks or chicken and dinner will be done without making a mess in the kitchen.

Easier Entertaining

Make a satisfying meal quickly and easily with almost no clean up. Just make a bunch of individual foil packets (one for each person) with a complete serving of meat and veggies. Grill 'em, serve 'em, and then just toss the foil when you're done. *(See Basil Chicken Packets, page 29.)*

Faster Fajitas

Craving fajitas? Grill marinated beef or chicken on one side of the grill while you cook up some onions and peppers in a packet or DIY Foil Grill Pan on the other. It tastes fantastic, it's a quick and easy way to get dinner on the table, and it's also a breeze to clean up afterwards.

Tastier Tortillas

Seal a stack of store-bought tortillas in a foil packet. Toss it on the grill (or bake in the oven if you're not cooking out). In a few minutes they'll be as warm and inviting as fresh, homemade tortillas.

BASIL CHICKEN PACKETS

4   sheets (12×18 inches each) REYNOLDS WRAP® Heavy
    Duty Foil

4   boneless, skinless chicken breast halves (1 to 1¼ pounds)

2   tablespoons chopped fresh parsley

2   to 3 teaspoons grated lemon peel

1½ teaspoons dried basil

½   teaspoon salt

2   medium yellow squash, sliced

1   medium red bell pepper, cut into rings

    Freshly ground black pepper to taste

Preheat grill to medium-high OR oven to 450°F.

Center one chicken breast half on each sheet of
Reynolds Wrap Heavy Duty Foil. Combine parsley, lemon peel,
basil and salt; sprinkle over chicken. Top with squash and bell
pepper. Sprinkle with black pepper.

Bring up foil sides. Double fold top and ends to seal packet,
leaving room for heat circulation inside. Repeat to make four
packets.

Grill 11 to 13 minutes in covered grill or BAKE 16 to 18
minutes on a cookie sheet in oven.

Makes 4 servings

Really Great Ribs

Make the most incredibly tender ribs ever by starting them in foil packets on the grill. Tightly seal racks (or half racks) in individual foil packets and grill them until they're just about done. Then just pull them from the packets, glaze them with your favorite barbecue sauce, and finish them over direct heat on the grill. *(See Baby Back Barbecue Ribs, page 31.)*

Ensure Even Cooking

Loosely wrapping or covering with foil any food that is getting too brown too quickly helps shield the exterior from excess direct heat while allowing the cooking process to continue. It's your best bet to prevent food from being overcooked outside and undercooked inside.

Cook Ahead for Tomorrow

You've already got the grill good and hot for tonight's dinner, so why not get a head start on tomorrow's? Grill extra burgers, chicken, or steak; cool. Wrap tightly in foil and refrigerate for use in salads, stir-fries or sandwiches.

BABY BACK BARBECUE RIBS

2   sheets (18×24 inches each) REYNOLDS WRAP® Heavy
      Duty Foil

3   pounds baby back pork ribs

1   tablespoon packed brown sugar

1   tablespoon paprika

2   teaspoons garlic powder

1½ teaspoons pepper

½   cup water or 6 to 8 ice cubes, divided

1½ cups barbecue sauce

Preheat grill to medium.

Center half of ribs on each sheet of Reynolds Wrap Heavy
Duty Foil. Combine brown sugar and spices; rub over ribs,
turning to coat evenly.

Bring up foil sides. Double fold top and one end to seal
packet. Through open end, add ¼ cup of water or 3 to 4
ice cubes. Double fold remaining end, leaving room for heat
circulation inside. Repeat to make two packets.

Grill for 45 to 60 minutes in covered grill. Remove ribs from
foil; place ribs on grill.

Brush ribs with barbecue sauce. Continue grilling 10 to 15
minutes, brushing with sauce and turning every 5 minutes.

Makes 5 to 6 servings

Chapter 4

Travel

These days traveling right means traveling light, and that means choosing travel accessories that are as versatile as they are useful. You already know a little Reynolds Wrap® Foil can go a long way in helping you keep food fresh and tasty while you're traveling the highways—but don't stop there. After keeping your sandwich fresh and tasty, the foil can be easily smoothed out to make a place mat or platter for a snack or impromptu picnic at any convenient roadside park. Foil can be handy in any number of other ways, too, such as helping to identify luggage at the airport and helping you pack efficiently.

Road Trip Rules

Keeping a roll of foil in your car helps to keep you moving during a car trip by reducing the reasons you need to stop.

Heat and Eat

 Foods well wrapped in foil can be warmed up quickly just by laying the package on a warm engine or grill for a few minutes. Seal food to be heated tightly in a double layer of foil and keep it chilled in a cooler. Ready for lunch? Reheat laying on any flat, warm surface under the hood for a few minutes on each side. Kids love to know their lunch was "cooked" on the engine of the family car!

Road Trip Refuse

Keep a roll of foil in your car to collect scraps of snacks and discarded items as they accumulate during long rides. You'll never wonder where to safely stash the kids' used tissues again.

Emergency Rain Hat

Stuck in the rain without an umbrella? Grab a sheet of foil to wrap around your head. It could serve as an impromptu shower cap, too.

Instant Place Mat

One of many kids' favorite things about road trips are all the great snacking opportunities. To keep your little ones' laps clean and dry during snack time, tear off a long sheet (18 inches or so) of foil and lay it across their laps before handing out snacks. Snack time over? Your kids can seal up their leftovers and save them for later, or wrap up any trash to contain it (with no mess or spills) until you can properly dispose of it.

Emergency Signal

There are few things quite so terrifying as being stuck on the side of a highway in the dark of night because of car problems. A few sheets of foil hung from a window or two help reflect the headlights of oncoming traffic making your car more visible to other drivers and helping to keep you safe until roadside assistance arrives.

PACKED WITH USEFUL IDEAS

Ready for adventure? Reynolds Wrap Foil is! Whether you're traveling across town or crossing oceans, be sure to bring foil along.

Easily Identify Luggage

Luggage looks so much alike nowadays. To separate your bags from the crowd, tightly wrap a piece of foil around the handle of your luggage. Your suitcase will be so easy to identify as it arrives on the baggage carousel.

Wet Bathing Suits

Enjoy one last dip in the pool without worrying about having to pack dripping wet swimsuits and beach towels. Once you've changed back into dry clothes, wring as much water out of your wet things as you can. Fold neatly and wrap them tightly in foil. Then pack them with the rest of your stuff without soaking everything!

Protect Books

Foil makes a perfect temporary cover for books. It not only keeps the book clean but also protects the binding from heat and water.

Perfect Packing

Trying to consolidate luggage into one bag and don't want shoes next to your good dress? Wrap shoes in foil to protect against dirt and odors.

Save Foil Package Cores

 The cores of the foil cartons can be used, too. Save them to place in the folds of garments when packed to protect from sharp creases.

BETTER BOXED LUNCHES

Whether you're road-tripping to Grandma's house, brown-bagging it at the office, or packing a meal for your school-aged child, lunch travels well when wrapped in foil.

Lunches Wrapped in Foil Stay Fresher

 Sandwiches don't dry out and raw vegetables stay crisp. And as an added bonus used foil can be recycled.

Foil Doubles as a Place Mat

Foil not only holds sandwiches together and keeps them fresh, it also makes a great place mat when unfolded. It acts as a clean, protective barrier between your food and cafeteria table or desktop surfaces.

Freeze Ahead Lunch Box Treats

 Bake brownies, cookies, or bars. Wrap them individually in foil and freeze. Pop a frozen treat into the lunch box in the morning, and it will be defrosted by lunchtime.

Prevent Soggy Sandwiches

 If you send tomato and lettuce, wrap them separately in foil and have your student add them to the sandwich at lunchtime.

Packing Fruits and Veggies

 Peeled baby carrots and a container of low-fat ranch dressing are an easy healthy choice. For variety, slice up a rainbow of peppers, celery, broccoli, or cauliflower and wrap in foil.

Show You Care

 Send a special note to your child in their lunch box. Wrap a treat or sandwich in foil and use a permanent marker to write your note right on the foil. (Even as kids get older and don't really want to admit it, they enjoy a word of encouragement during their day!)

Chapter 5

Camping

Whether you're trekking through the back country or just going down to the local park for a cookout, tuck a roll of Reynolds Wrap® Foil in your pack and you're ready for all sorts of adventures in the great outdoors.

Tear off sheets to protect precious items no matter where you set them down. Foil is great to have on hand when you're cooking over a campfire, and you can also use it to make disposable cookware and plates, to wrap and preserve left-overs, or to create a clean, dry place to set cooking utensils while preparing meals.

CAMPSITE COOKING

Foil is useful for so much more than just wrapping leftovers at your campsite. Save yourself the hassle of packing and cleaning campsite cookware by making single use pans out of foil.

Foil Skillet

 For a quick campsite frying pan, center a forked stick on 2 layered sheets of foil each about twice as long as the distance between the two prongs of the stick. Wrap the foil over the stick and crimp tightly in place. Prop the pan over hot embers by resting it on rocks.

Canteen Cups

 It only takes a moment to shape foil into a drinking cup so you can share a cool drink of water with a friend and no one has to drink from the bottle or canteen.

Cookware-Free Foods

 Wrap potatoes, squash, corn, or apples completely in foil and place in glowing embers. Using tongs or a few thick sticks, roll to a new side every few minutes until soft but not mushy. Roll out of the embers and let cool before removing the foil and enjoying a roasted treat.

Perfect Burgers

It's easy to shape perfect-size hamburgers with a foil hamburger press. Fold a 12-inch sheet of foil into a 2-inch-wide band. Crimp the ends of the band together to make a 3-inch circle. Pat ground beef in ring to shape; remove ring to cook.

Burgers on the Go

Season, shape, and wrap individual burgers in foil before leaving home, and freeze solid. Carry frozen burgers to the campsite in a cooler where they can help keep the rest of your meal cold as they thaw in time for you to grill.

Sweet Finish

Don't forget a little dessert! Stack a piece of a chocolate bar and a marshmallow between two pieces or graham cracker and wrap it up the next time you're cooking out. *(See Easy Grilled S'mores, page 41.)*

CAMP GEAR PROTECTION

Use a large piece of foil as protection from damp ground or surfaces.

EASY GRILLED S'MORES

4   sheets (8×12-inches each) REYNOLDS WRAP® Heavy Duty Foil

4   graham crackers, broken in halves

2   milk chocolate candy bars (1.55 oz. each), divided in half crosswise

4   large marshmallows

Preheat grill to medium. For each S'more, top one graham cracker square with one candy bar half, one marshmallow and another graham cracker square. Repeat with remaining graham crackers, candy and marshmallows.

Center one S'more on each sheet of Reynolds Wrap Heavy Duty Foil. Bring up foil sides. Double fold top and ends to seal packet, leaving room for heat circulation inside. Repeat to make four packets.

Grill 4 to 5 minutes in covered grill.

Makes 4 servings

Equipment

Preserve and protect electronic equipment (such as a radio or camera) by placing it on a sheet of foil or by wrapping the bottom in a layer of foil before setting it on the ground.

Sleep Easy

A layer of foil between your sleeping bag and the floor of your tent can help you sleep safe and sound without worrying about wet or frozen ground outside.

Chapter 6

Hobby & Workbench

Having the right tool is an essential part of doing a job right, and Reynolds Wrap® Foil an essential tool in every well-stocked tool kit. When used properly, it not only helps get the job done right, but preserves and protects the other tools you use, too. Keep a roll handy on your workbench, in the garage, or wherever you work hard and get your chores done.

And when you're done working hard, foil can play an important role in fostering creative activities and hobbies of all sorts.

MESS-FREE PAINT HELPER

What's the most handy tool for do-it-yourself painters? Foil, of course!

Keep Paintbrushes Ready

Paintbrushes stay soft when wrapped in foil. Cleaning or soaking is eliminated—perfect for when you need to stop painting before you're finished.

Clean Paint Pans

For easy cleanup, line your paint roller pans with foil. When you've finished painting, simply throw away the foil, leaving a clean paint roller pan for the next project.

Save Paint

To prevent "skin" from forming in an opened paint can, lay a circle of foil right on the paint surface.

Avoid Paint Splatters

Before you start painting, wrap doorknobs or other hard-to-remove accessories with foil to protect them from paint splatters and drips.

HOBBY KNOW-HOW

Whatever your hobby, foil can help keep things neat and clean or lend a special sparkle.

Scrapbooking with Foil

 Why buy expensive scrapbooking paper when you can make your own? Emboss foil by rubbing a sheet of foil over a texture such as carpet, tile, or even a notebook cover. Use the embossed foil as a scrapbook page background or around a photo.

Scrapbooking Embellishments

Make your scrapbook pages shine with foil embellishments. Names or letters can be embossed in foil by rubbing over baby blocks. Make corner decorations by gluing string onto pages in fun designs. Press foil over design and glue in place.

Sharpen Paper Punches

Decorative paper punches for crafting or 3-hole punches at the office can be sharpened by punching through several layers of foil.

Heat Protector for Glue Gun

 Place a hot glue gun on a sheet of foil to protect surfaces. Foil takes the heat and catches any stray drips of hot glue.

WORKBENCH WONDERS

Keep an extra roll of foil in the garage or on the workbench to aid in projects around the house.

Protect Seldom-Used Tools

 Between uses, oil your tools and wrap them in foil to keep them from rusting.

Smooth Snow Shoveling

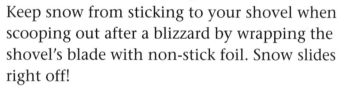 Keep snow from sticking to your shovel when scooping out after a blizzard by wrapping the shovel's blade with non-stick foil. Snow slides right off!

Trash Can Saver

Line the bottoms of metal trash cans with circles of foil to prevent the can from rusting. The foil can be easily replaced when soiled.

Chapter 7

Gardening

Reynolds Wrap® Foil is so versatile you're bound to find uses for it in almost every room in your house, so it should come as no surprise to find several uses *outside* your house, too. There are few tools available to gardeners that match foil's flexibility and durability. It's easy to mold foil into custom-shaped pots and mats—and since it's waterproof, rustproof, and sterile, it's perfect for starting seeds to be transplanted later. It's also helpful when growing indoor potted plants and arranging cut flowers.

OUTDOOR GARDENING

Add a roll of foil to your gardening tools to make the most of your outdoor plantings.

Plant Starters

 Start seedlings indoors to be transplanted to the garden later in cups formed from foil and filled with potting or garden soil. When the plants are big enough to set out, tear the foil away, lift out the seedling, and plant in the garden.

Easy "Mulch"

 Mulch your garden with strips of foil. Laid between rows or around single plants, the foil repels aphids, holds moisture in the ground, reflects sun rays, and prevents weeds. Just anchor the foil with a little loose soil.

Frost Shield

 A cover of foil protects plants from frost. Large sheets can be used for a large planting and small hot caps for small plants.

Plant Protection

 Protect plant stems from cutworms and insects by wrapping them in foil.

Protect Young Trees

 To keep rabbits and other animals from eating the bark of young trees, wrap the lower two or three feet of the trunk with a double layer of foil. Fasten the foil securely with string or moisture-proof tape.

Graft Trees

 Foil can be used as a sterile cover for the joined area when grafting a limb onto a host plant, to protect a damaged section of bark, and to wrap limbs split by wind or snow loads.

INDOOR FLOWERS AND PLANTS

Protect and nurture potted plants with foil. It's also handy to have on hand when arranging cut flowers to fill a vase or a bouquet.

Protect Tables and Sills

Cut foil in attractive patterns and place under potted plants to protect tables and window sills.

Revitalize Your Vases

A cracked vase can still be used if you line it with foil to keep the water from seeping through the crack.

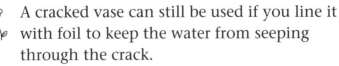

Beautiful Bouquets

 Don't have an extra vase? Wrap flower stems in damp paper towels and over-wrap with foil to transport flowers to a friend's house.

Extended Usage

If a vase is too deep for the stems of your flowers, crumple foil in the bottom of the vase to hold up the flowers and provide extra height.

Winter Sunlight Reflector

Make the most out of what little sunlight you receive in winter. Place sheets of foil behind house plants to bathe plants in sunlight from both sides. This also helps prevent the plant from leaning toward the sun.

Chapter 8

Decorating

Many people are so familiar with the strength and security with which Reynolds Wrap® Foil wraps and protects things that they tend to overlook the natural decorative qualities of shiny, sparkly foil. Just a few pieces of foil used to trim a holiday decoration is often all it takes to make a run-of-the-mill holiday display seem extraordinary.

Make room for foil on your holiday table, too. Use it to decorate a wreath, or to create a home-made holiday card.

MAKE PARTY TABLES SHINE

Use foil to create dishes and serving pieces when you don't have the right size or shape.

Decorative Trays

Cover round or oval cardboard shapes with foil to make decorative trays for everything from vegetables to cakes.

Serving Sub Sandwiches

Need a serving board for a super-size sub sandwich? Place magazines end to end and tape together. Cover the entire length with foil.

Cups of All Sizes and Shapes

Foil can be molded into an endless variety of cups to hold nuts or candy on a tray. Great for entertaining, for portion control, or to make a single-serving dish for children.

Lost Cork

Lost the cork but don't want to finish a bottle of wine? Crumple foil into a replacement cork large enough to fit the bottle, leaving enough sticking out to remove easily.

SPARKLING SILVER DECORATIONS

Whatever the occasion, affordable decorations can be fashioned with foil and a little imagination.

Star-Bright

 For your next "out-of-this-world" theme party for kids, cut several sizes of stars, moons, and other astronomic shapes from sturdy cardboard. Cover with foil (shiny side out, of course). Great for homecoming and prom decorations, too.

Children's Party Place Mats

 Make customized place mats for a children's party. Cut cardboard mats in different shapes or letters and cover them with foil.

Silver Celebrations

 Planning a silver anniversary, engagement, or holiday party? Foil makes perfect decorations thanks to its silvery shine.

Thanksgiving Cornucopia

 Create a beautiful cornucopia centerpiece by covering a cone-shaped piece of cardboard with foil and then crushing the cone into the horn shape.

CANDLE MAGIC

Light dances when reflected by foil and protects tables and surfaces, too.

Candle Wax Protection

 Cut foil in floral patterns with a hole in the center and slip over candles to dress up the holder and catch drips.

Prevent Wobbly Candles

 Fold or crinkle foil around bottom of candles to keep them upright in candlesticks.

PLAY CLOTHES AND COSTUMES

Use foil to create custom costumes or accessories for Halloween, costume parties or when the kids want to play dress up.

Custom Costumes

 Foil is great for accessorizing obvious costumes like the Tin Man or a robot, but try adding foil to superhero, astronauts, kings and queens, angels, candy kisses or stars.

Faux Silver Jewelry

Roll foil into ropes and form into bracelets, necklaces, belts or rings. Works great for hats and hair bows, too.

GREAT GIFT GIVING

Use foil to add a personal touch to last-minute gifts and cards.

Gift Boxes

 Recycled old boxes become part of beautiful gifts when neatly covered with foil.

Gift Wrap

 Out of regular wrapping paper? Gifts wrapped in foil glisten and reflect colored lights when placed under the Christmas tree.

Gorgeous Gift Tags

Make any shape gift tag from foil. Fold a piece of foil in half and cut out a silhouette, leaving one side uncut, so that the tag will open like a book. Trace onto a piece of paper then cut out and glue paper inside the foil.

Holiday Cards

 Children and adults alike will enjoy the original and lovely holiday cards that can be made with foil as a background.

Holiday Food Gifts

 Baked goods make tasty gifts in boxes or tins lined with foil. Wrap with foil to keep them fresh, too.

CHRISTMAS DECORATIONS

Beautiful, shimmering Christmas ornaments and decorations can be cut and shaped from foil. Here, the imagination knows no bounds.

Mini Christmas Trees

 A miniature Christmas tree made from graduated tiers of foil can grace your table as a centerpiece.

Christmas Tree Stand

 Foil at the base of the tree covers the stem and tree stand, and provides the perfect setting for gifts or Christmas scenes. Covering the tree skirt means easy cleanup of dry needles.

Christmas Tree Light Reflector

 Reflectors for Christmas tree lights are very simple to make. Cut squares of foil with holes in the middle. Insert the bulb through the hole and fan the foil out from the light.

Outdoor Decorations

 A foil bow on an outdoor wreath will remain fresh and bright long after cloth ribbons have wilted from exposre to the weather.

Chapter 9

Household

Want a little extra help around the house? Take a roll of Reynolds Wrap® Foil out of the kitchen and you'll discover a whole world of new uses. There are practical applications for foil in every room of the house. Use it to help press clean clothes in your laundry room, or to organize clothes in your closet. You can use it to protect furniture or make the most of your fireplace. There are even roles foil can play in organizing your medicine cabinet or bathroom drawers.

HOUSEHOLD USES

Sharpen Your Scissors

 Sharpen your scissors simply by cutting through six to eight layers of foil.

Quick Silver Cleaning

 Here's the quickest way to polish silver: Place a large piece of foil in the bottom of a glass pan; add silver to be cleaned. In a large pot, mix 2 tablespoons baking soda and 2 quarts of water. Bring to boil. Pour over silver, covering completely. Let stand for a few minutes. Remove the silver—it will now be bright and shiny—and wash in hot sudsy water. Rinse well, dry thoroughly, then polish with a soft dry cloth. Once you've cleaned the silver, wrap seldom-used pieces in foil to keep them from tarnishing.

Stop Loose Windows

 Insert foil into the cracks between a window and its sill to keep drafts out and keep the windows from rattling when the wind blows.

Furniture Protector

 Place small pieces of foil under furniture legs to protect them from moisture damage when you shampoo your rugs and carpets.

Clean Closets

 Keep dresses or shirts with spaghetti straps from landing on the closet floor by covering hangers with foil. Form a lump in the foil to catch the straps. Works great for scoop-neck shirts, too!

CARING FOR CLOTHES

Foil can help protect and care for your family's clothing.

Speedy Wrinkle Remover

Foil placed between the pad and cover on an ironing board reflects heat and saves ironing time. The foil prevents steam from going into the pad, helps moisten the fabric being ironed, and removes wrinkles quickly.

Easy Clothes Steamer

Remove wrinkles from silk or clothes that can't take direct heat. Place foil on ironing board and lay garment over foil. With steam button down, pass iron 3 to 4 inches over fabric several times.

Missing Shoelace Tip

 Lost the tip of your shoelace? Cover the end of the shoelace with foil and rethread through eyelets.

Quick Fixes for Torn Jeans

Ripped jeans may be in fashion for teens, but for tears that need a quick fix, iron-on patches are just the thing. Place a piece of foil under the garment before ironing on the patch. The foil concentrates the heat and keeps the patch from sticking to the ironing board cover.

HEARTH SIDE

Fireplace Aids

Line the bottom of the fireplace fire box with foil to catch ashes. The foil lining and ashes can be removed in one step for easy cleanup.

Fireplace Liner

Fireplaces lined with foil will reflect more heat and use less fuel.

Chapter 10

Thrifty Ideas

Reynolds Wrap® Foil can help you make the most of your food budget by making sure the foods you buy are wrapped and stored properly. Dry air in the freezer, and even any excess air trapped inside packages of food, can draw moisture out of food and cause frost and freezer burn. Save even more money by replacing store-bought frozen dinners with more wholesome homemade options. Foil-wrapped food is ready to go from freezer to oven and then straight to the table without even dirtying a pan.

FROZEN FUNDS

Packages tightly wrapped in foil instead of placed in plastic containers save space in the freezer and allow you to store foods closer together (which helps your freezer operate more efficiently, too).

How to Wrap Food for Freezing

Protect food against freezer burn by molding heavy duty foil tightly to the food and pressing out excess air.

1. Center food on a sheet of foil large enough for adequate wrapping.
2. Bring long sides of foil together over food.
3. Fold foil down in tight folds, pressing out excess air. Fold up short ends.
4. Label, date, and freeze foil package.

Squish-Free Freezer

Protect soft foods such as baked goods or cooked fish by first freezing them in a single, unwrapped layer just until frozen solid (usually an hour or two). Remove the fully frozen items from the freezer, wrap, and then return to the freezer until needed.

Cook Once, Eat Twice

Double your savings on time and meals by double batching. Make your favorite recipes in casseroles lined with foil; serve one casserole and cover, label, and freeze the second one, using the casserole wrap technique *(see below)*.

How to Freeze Casseroles

1. Line pans with enough heavy duty foil to extend up over the edges. To line pans easily, turn pan upside down. Press foil over the outside of the inverted pan. Remove foil. Flip pan over and drop shaped foil inside.
2. Crimp edges of foil to rim of pan. Add food.
3. Cover with a top sheet of foil. Crimp foil edges together and freeze.
4. When frozen, remove the pan and return the sealed foil package to the freezer.
5. To reheat, place foil package back into original baking pan. Uncover and bake.

Freezer-Ready Breakfast

Make extra pancakes and waffles when you have time. Wrap in foil and freeze. To reheat, pop them in the oven or toaster for a few minutes.

Buy Meats on Sale

 Save money by shopping smart. Buy large quantities of meat when it's on sale, wrap meal-size portions and freeze in foil. Seal meat (in its original packaging) in foil for fresher frozen foods.

SAVE THE SECOND TIME, TOO

Saving leftovers saves you money, but only if you keep them fresh and ready to eat. Tightly wrapping foods in foil prevents them from going stale as quickly in the refrigerator.

Take-Out Times Two

 Next time you buy take-out or delivered food, order enough for two meals. Wrap the second meal in foil and freeze. It'll save you a stop for food next time you're in a hurry. Foil-wrapped leftovers stay more appetizing for longer in the fridge, too.

Leftover Pasta Makes Tomorrow's Salad

Top pasta with just about anything and you have an instant meal. When you're cooking pasta, cook a double amount. Serve half the pasta for dinner tonight. Toss the leftover pasta with a little olive oil or sesame oil. Cover with foil and refrigerate for a great start on tomorrow's pasta salad.

Leftovers Make Tomorrow's Dinner Easy

Portion leftovers on individual plates for each person; cover with foil and refrigerate. Family members eating on varying schedules can uncover and reheat in the microwave when ready.

Refresh Bread and Rolls

Freshen stale bread, rolls, or doughnuts by sprinkling them with a few drops of water, wrapping them in foil, and heating them in a 400°F oven for 5 to 10 minutes or until warm.

Eliminate Extra Baking Pans

Wrap leftovers to be frozen or refrigerated in foil. When you're ready to reheat them, they can go directly from the freezer or refrigerator to the oven. Place a cookie sheet under each foil package for support.